The Absolute Best
Little Book Of Poetry

Dannette Stevens

ISBN 978-1-0980-6190-6 (paperback)
ISBN 978-1-0980-4891-4 (hardcover)
ISBN 978-1-0980-4892-1 (digital)

Christian Faith Publishing, Inc.
832 Park Avenue
Meadville, PA 16335
www.christianfaithpublishing.com

Printed in the United States of America

Hurt and Heavenly Hope
Now That's Dope

They wanted it to hurt
They threw their dirt.
I felt the pain; I saw their shame.
I remain the same, unchanged, unbothered because of my Father.

God Given Dreams

Dreams, vivid, lucid, crystal clear, don't you dare live in fear.
Get up! Get out! Time has not run out.
Give God a great shout after all this is what life is all about!
Let everything that has breath praise the Lord.
Lead me, guide me, shepherd me to my destiny.
Thank you for the dreams you placed in my heart, and now it's
    time for
Me to do my part!

There is Power in the name of Jesus

What are these chains that enslave me?
How could this be?
How did it happen to me?
The weight of the world… "What's up with you girl?" I said to
    myself.
I'm not feeling like me. Oh, how could this be?
I opened my mouth and called out his name…
He broke every chain.
JESUS

Family
Little Is Much as long as God Is in It

When we had nothing,
We had everything.
Now we have everything
And we have nothing.

Pain and the Joy of the Lord Is My Strength

I felt the hurt in my stomach
I felt it in my throat
My body ached, and my mind raced
Everything was a bother
It was a dark place and empty space.
I wish it could all be erased.
It made me stronger.
It made me hunger for brighter days.
And just like that God lifted that haze, and I was amazed.

No Snake, No Garden

This one's for you
You laughed, and I stood
You tried and lied…
And still I thrived and then multiplied.
This one's for you and all that you do!
My dreams still came true!
No snake, no garden.

Train Up a Child

I wish I could protect you all the days of your life, but you must
grow and go your way.
And if I have done my part, God will always be the center of
your heart.
"Train up a child in the way he should go. And when he is old
he will not depart from it" (Proverbs 22:6).

Stagnation and Elevation

The waiting place
A slow pace
You must take a position
Hot or cold, lukewarm just won't do
Pray and press, press and pray forward to a brand new day...
    for your
Blessing is just a day away.

Tears

Tears wet and warm, they run like streams and storms.
Tears a release and relief from all life's grief.
Tears are meant to make you grow and not to keep you feeling low.
So go and grow and let those tears go.

Get Back Up Again

The pitfall was meant for us all.
The pitiful place, the place where sorrows run deep, and there
   is no sleep.
But when just one sheep was lost, he bore it all on the cross.
He died for our sins so we could live again. Amen.
So when you're feeling blue and don't know what to do,
Get back up again.
When your crown is lost and your feeling tossed,
Get back up again.
You can begin again, just get back up again.

Distractions

Distractions and reactions.

I pray, dear Lord, I pass this test because these distractions don't give a rest. At my best in this game of chess, you, dear Lord, give me rest.

Guard my tongue and my thoughts too because I want to be with you.

The Steps of a Righteous Man Are Ordered by God

I remember that day running the track with you as I always do.
Picking up the pace in this familiar place we call time and space.
If only I could run this race at a much quicker pace, then maybe I
wouldn't have to face your speculations, my hesitations and
    friends'
exhortations. Yet here we are, you and I running this race at a
    slow but
steady pace.

Hallelujah

Life and Liberty in Christ

The world's system is not for me!
You see, I am free.
Free from all the expectations and explanations the world has
of me.
I'll run this race at my own pace.
I walk to the beat of a different drum, and if you like, you can
come.
I am not done; the world has yet to see the best of me
For what God has for me is life more abundantly.

Open Doors

Just put one foot in front of the other and soon you will dis-
    cover a
Love unlike any other. Just put one foot in front of the other and
Watch your dreams come true. What you have to do is think it
through and through. Then put one foot in front of the other and
Watch him do for you what no mortal man can do.

Joy

Joy like a beautiful sunset that feels warm, wonderful, and wet.
Joy like a hundred kisses and Christmases.
Joy like a beautiful day at the beach or a goal you once thought
    was out
of reach. Joy like a sermon that was just preached that touched
    you oh
so deep because you were once the lost sheep. Joy until the day you
lost it and felt accosted. Never to take you for granted again.
    Joy, you
are my friend.

Hallelujah

Memories

(To Be Absent in the Body Is to Be Present with the Lord)

I remember the day that you went away; it hurt so bad inside.
You were the one God gave me to raise me, and I was your baby.
I will see you again in those pearly gates and run into your arms,
Marvel in all your charms just as I did when I was a kid.
Until then, I'll be strong for it won't be long, and I'll be back in
Daddy's arms.

Mother

You reared me and steered me
You taught me and bought me
You showed me and told me
You held me, you hugged me and love me
You clocked me and rocked me
You surprise me and advise me
You tell me I am your own, for this, you deserve a throne.
A queen and her court, you have my support.
Mother, like none other...
I love her.

Destiny

Destiny is not a place, it's a journey and if that is true, I'd like to journey with you. They thought all was lost when you died on that cross, but your destiny was to reconcile me. You paid a high price just
to save my life. As I ponder on my destiny, I won't let the enemy get the best of me. I remind myself you died for my wealth, and I shall recover it all.

Best Friend

A true friend is a blessing, and that's what you are to me.
I won't leave you behind; the two of us have a special bond.
You are the iron that sharpens me, and I the same to thee.
Where you go, I'll follow and defend you to the end because
    you are
My best friend.

Temptation

Temptation, temptation, oh, the elation and sensation you bring.
But what seems so small could cause a great fall and run the
    risk of
Losing it all. So I walk the straight and narrow despite the dark
Arrows.

Glory

Glory is when I'll see you in those heavenly lights.
Glory is when you visit me late at night.
Glory is to behold the most beautiful sight.
Glory is when you make everything terrible all right.
Glory is when you turned the darkness to light.
Glory, glory all through the day and night.

Magical Moments with Christ

Have you ever had one of those moments you just can't explain
  left
You changed. While riding the train, I had one of those
  moments.
I was seeking his face no matter the place; I was on a chase.
I needed to see him with haste. Then came a light upon my face
  went
through my body, and I knew it was him, left me shaken, there
  was no
mistaken it was him. Come see me again; until then, I'll wait
  on my
next magical moment with him.

Sunshine

Warm as the ray
Clear as the day
Bright bursts of colorful marmalade and a cool drink in the shade
Iridescent, candescent, fluorescent, I never want to lose your
essence.
Sunshine, you are mine.

Golden

Turn up the fire, turn up the flame
I am ready for a change
Singe me anew, I want to be like you
No matter the cost, I want to be golden because I am beholden of
Every promise spoken, so if I must be broken, let me be your token
Turn up the flame, I need a change.

Snow

White as the snow
An angel all a glow
You are so pure coming down from the sky
Snow and your magnificent lights make bright the dark nights.

Rumors

(No Weapons Formed Against Me Shall Prosper)

Don't let rumors ruin a good thing.
Rumors and there ugly sting give the gossipers a great ting.
Don't let rumors have the last word.
Am I being heard, don't give me the last word.

Love

Love like a cozy sweater full of down feathers
Love like the deepest river or the highest mountain
Love like you can't escape it because it engulfs you and all that you
do. Love like you never want it to go away because you never know
When it is your last day to say I love you.

Rainbow People

Rainbow people, God created us equal.
I see your colors and traditions too
That's what makes you uniquely you
So why do we fight over a ridiculous plight when we are all
    precious in
His sight. Rainbow people, when will you understand there's no
Difference in a man.

Promises of God

I remember my mother saying I'm standing on the promises of
   God.
I'm holding tight with all my spiritual might.
I'm waiting on the promises of God, for I know his word is true.
   It will
Perform exactly what it set out to do. I'm sure I'll be surprised
   on the
Day his word arrives; you'll know by the look in my eyes.
I'm standing on the promises of God.

Hopeful

How did we lose our way saying things we should not say?
Looking forward to a better day.
Hoping we can both forgive, and forget is really our best bet.
Hurt has never solved any problems yet.
Looking forward to a better day is all that I can say.

The Pitiful Place and God's Amazing Grace

I was covered in sin, oh, where shall I begin.
My faith was dim. and folks say my chances are slim.
But there in the darkest place was God's amazing grace.
A heart full of gold and the lover of my soul.
He filled that empty space with his amazing grace.
The pitiful place has been erased without a trace of sin, his
   blood has me born again.
The rest is history, so long misery.
I'll be basking in that secret place called his amazing grace.

God Is Love

Love like the most beautiful song you want to rock to all day long.
Love like your first kiss, the one you always reminisce.
Love like a beautiful breeze that blows through the forest and trees.
Whatever you do, do it in love, so your father above gets all the
    glory
End of story.

Saved

I am saved, signed, sealed and delivered from the bottomless
    pit and
From all the enemies' tricks. Happily his, I'm saved to see
    another day
May my father have his way. A day to praise his holy name and
    thank
Him just the same. Hallelujah, I am saved. All praises to the
    most high
For setting me aside.

Gifts

Gifts that were meant to behold
A story that was meant to be told
God makes space for your place
You're never too young or to old
Just listen to what's deep in your soul.

Past

We all have a past so please don't ask, just accept me for who I am.
I've learned from my past mistakes, and I got what it takes to
    make it
In this Life. So do me a favor, don't go ask my neighbor, just
    accept me
For who I am.

Faith

When it all began, I had a plan, and it was just me and hope.
Faith planted a seed, and now my every need has been met with
good
Deeds. So I'm keeping the faith like you keep a keepsake.

Forgiveness

How could we lose what we did not choose? Blood made us
    family so
Why can't we get back to amicably? If we dare to care and
    beware of
Our words, we can get back to place we once knew where everyone
Was true blue. I don't care what we heard, and I know that's
Absurd, but I give you my word. Let's start anew, family… I
    love you.

New Beginnings

Like every seed that drops from a tree so shall we begin again.
God's rest has you blessed and carried you through the mess.
In the still of the night, he blessed you with spiritual sight.
You can begin again.
Adopted you into the family and taught you his ways all for
   you to
Get to brighter days. You can begin again. He married you in
   spite of
Your sins so that you could begin again.

Dear Brothers

Brother, I really thought back then you were a bother. You would
Make a fuss when it was just us. But in you, I've learned to trust
Because you always protected us. My big brother, what can I
    say, you
Were always there to make my day. Look down on you never;
    you are
Always so clever. So like birds of a feather, we will always be
    together.

Dear Sister

Did I ever tell you how much you meant to me? You have a
  heart of
Gold such a peaceful soul. When we get together, we are a pos-
  itive force
Moving along the same course. When I am with you, I feel like
  I can
Move mountains. I am stronger. Every time you visit, I wish it
  could be
Longer. Nothing could ever keep us apart you will be forever
  in my
heart.

In a Perfect World

In a perfect world, there's no hatred, and everyone is sacred.
Love would ebb and flow, and no one would care to know
  about your
Financial status or any of your old proclivities or new activities.
In a perfect world, there'd be no need for a sequel. All girls and boys
Would be equal. In a perfect world, love would reign supreme,
  and I wish
This weren't just a dream.

The Throne

You alone in the darkness of time and space, there upon your
    throne of
Grace. You separated the heavens from the earth and then gave
    birth to
The first day. You sowed the seeds of mankind, and now we
    reap time
After time. There you are in the mercy seat as we lay our troubles at
Your feet.

Warnings

Warnings come to let us know there are times to take it slow.
Listen not with your natural ears but to the heart that hears
    that still
Voice in your ears. Know this voice is not based on fears, your
Emotions or tears. You will know it when you hear the Holy
    Spirit is
Near.

Holy, Holy

Holy, Holy Spirit, you are welcome here. Come close, be with
  me. You
See all that I can be. Holy, Holy Spirit, how you lead me and
  keep me
From harm. I am surrounded by goodness and light and the
  power of
Your might. I feel your presence all around me and everywhere
  I go.
Help me in every area of my life, especially in the areas I have
  strife.
Holy, Holy Spirit, you are welcome here.

Marriage

When a man finds a wife, he finds a good thing. Despite what the
World may say, we know marriage is the best way. May our
    hearts
Never stray; I pledge my love today. May we always understand
    God
Is not a man. He holds our lives in his hands. Dear Lord, we
    give praises
To you for our marriage and all that you do.

Birth

I am pregnant with your word. It took hold in my womb and
   soon and
Very soon, I will give birth to what you instilled in my heart.
   May we
Never ever part. It took some time to bring you here. I poured my
Heart out year after year. Just know that you are very dear.
   Maybe it
Was fear or worry about what you'd hear. Maybe just
   procrastination
Or hesitation. I had to let that go so that I could grow. Grow
   in faith to
Bring you to fruition. This is my God-given mission.

Earth

For what it's worth, God gave us this green earth to cultivate and
Procreate. To spread your word like a turtledove and bless this
    earth
With lots of love.

Advice

Thanks for your advice. I'll be sure to think twice.
Watch where you receive advice.
People practice what you preach; your reach is kind of weak.
Your voice is kind of meek, and your advice, I did not seek.

Peace

(The Peace That Surpasses All Understanding)

All I want is peace.

The peace that gets down deep and affords a good night's sleep.

The peace that the world does not know but would set the world a glow.

Peace in our neighborhood streets and peace in the Middle East.

Peace, everywhere I go, I want the world to know I am peace.

The Last

I saved the best for last
What a monumental task
The first shall be last, and the last shall be first. That's the way God's
Kingdom works. Do your best, forget the rest, remember God is there
Through every test.

Author's Note

It is my hope that you fully enjoyed this little book of the absolute best poetry. May you be blessed richly.

Yours in Christ,
Mrs. Stevens

About the Author

Dannette holds a bachelor's degree in communications from Temple University and a master's degree in Education from Saint Joseph's University, Philadelphia, Pennsylvania. Dannette is currently an elementary school teacher and motivational speaker. As a teacher, Dannette completed the training program of master educator (2018) awarded by the Franklin Institute of Philadelphia, Pennsylvania. She is a mentor teacher for the Camden City School District located in Camden, New Jersey. Dannette is an active member of the New Jersey Education Association (NJEA) and National Education Association (NEA) Unions. Dannette is also an active member of the National Association for the Advancement of Colored People (NAACP) Camden County East Branch. This book of poetry was written for anyone who has experienced life's ups and downs and wondered, where is God? This book gives confirmation that God is real and is in every detail, for if you seek him, you will find him.